Caring For Your Body

SLEEP

Written by
Rebecca Phillips-Bartlett

KidHaven PUBLISHING

Published in 2025 by
KidHaven Publishing, an Imprint of
Greenhaven Publishing, LLC
2544 Clinton St., Buffalo, NY 14224

Written by: Rebecca Phillips-Bartlett
Edited by: E.C. Andrews
Designed by: Ker Ker Lee

All facts, statistics, web addresses and URLs in this book were verified as valid and accurate at time of writing. No responsibility for any changes to external websites or references can be accepted by either the author or publisher.

Cataloging-in-Publication Data

Names: Phillips-Bartlett, Rebecca, 1999-.
Title: Sleep / Rebecca Phillips-Bartlett.
Description: Buffalo, NY : KidHaven Publishing, 2025. | Series: Caring for your body | Includes glossary and index.
Identifiers: ISBN 9781534548923 (pbk.) | | SBN 9781534548930 (library bound) | ISBN 9781534548947 (ebook)
Subjects: LCSH: Sleep--Juvenile literature. | Sleep--Physiological aspects--Juvenile literature. | Self-care, Health--Juvenile literature.
Classification: LCC QP425.P45 2025 | DDC 612.8'21--dc23

Manufactured in the United States of America

CPSIA compliance information: Batch #CW25KH
For further information contact Greenhaven Publishing LLC at 1-844-317-7404.

Please visit our website, www.greenhavenpublishing.com.
For a free color catalog of all our high-quality books, call toll free 1-844-317-7404 or fax 1-844-317-7405.

Photo Credits – Images are courtesy of Shutterstock.com. With thanks to Getty Images, Thinkstock Photo and iStockphoto.

Recurring images – davooda, IRINA SHI. Cover – Anny Sketches, fizkes. 4–5 – alexei_tm, Krakenimages.com. 6–7 – Gumpanat, kitty, Roman Samborskyiki. 8–9 – Anatoliy Karlyuk, Queenmoonlite Studio, Yuganov Konstantin. 10–11 – Africa Studio, AnyaPL, fizkes, MF production. 12–13 – MillaF, Pixel-Shot. 14–15 – Hananeko_Studio, Mangkorn Danggura, Oksana Mizina. 16–17 – bbernard, Chinnapong. 18–19 – fizkes, VGstockstudio. 20–21 – Prostock-studio, Q88. 22–23 – chomplearn, Denis Kuvaev, WBMUL.

CONTENTS

Words that look like this can be found in the glossary on page 24.

CARING FOR YOU

Your body is just one part of who you are. However, the way you take care of your body can have a big impact on the way you feel in your mind.

Taking time to look after yourself is called self-care.

Caring for your body can help you feel happier, healthier, and give you more energy to do the things you enjoy. Caring for your body is a great way to start taking care of yourself.

ALL ABOUT SLEEP

Everyone needs sleep. In fact, our bodies cannot work without it. Sleep is a type of rest. The amount of sleep you get can affect how you feel when you wake up.

Do you have any pets? They need plenty of sleep too!

Different people need different amounts of sleep. Most people spend around one-third of their lives asleep. That means someone who is 90 years old will have spent around 30 years asleep throughout their life!

WHY DO I NEED SLEEP?

Sleep gives your body time to rest and recover from the day. This helps keep your body strong enough to fight infections and keep you healthy.

Sleep also gives your mind a chance to understand everything that happened during the day.

Young people's bodies grow and change very quickly. You are constantly learning new things. Young people need more sleep than grown-ups because your bodies and brains are working so hard all the time.

WHAT HAPPENS WHEN I SLEEP?

When you first fall asleep, your heart, brain, and eye movements slow down.

Once you are in a deep sleep, your body refills its energy supply. It also fixes any cells that were harmed during the day.

Deep sleep is also when your brain sorts through information. This is very important for memory and learning.

The final stage of sleep is called REM sleep. This is when you might have a dream.

Have you ever had a dream? What was it about?

HOW MUCH SLEEP DO I NEED?

Different people need different amounts of sleep. However, most young people need around nine to twelve hours of sleep each night. Most grown-ups only need seven to nine hours of sleep.

Different people might feel sleepy at different times. This is partly because of something called a body clock. Even if your body clock tries to keep you awake, it is important to get plenty of sleep.

I'M TIRED!

If you feel tired, that is usually a sign that you have not had enough sleep. Not getting enough sleep can have lots of other effects too. You might feel stressed, anxious, sad, or grumpy.

Being tired can make it harder to deal with big feelings.

Being tired can make it harder to concentrate. You might forget things or make mistakes that you would not usually make. Being tired can even make you clumsier than usual.

Not getting enough sleep can make you feel unwell or sick.

I CAN'T SLEEP!

Sometimes it can be tricky to get to sleep, even when you are really tired. Having a bedtime routine can help. A routine means doing the same things every day.

A routine helps your body understand that these activities mean it is bedtime.

A bedtime routine might look like:

- Going to bed at the same time every day
- Getting into your pajamas and brushing your teeth
- Not using screens for at least one hour before bed

If your worries are making sleeping tricky, try talking to a trusted grown-up.

WHY DO I DREAM?

Scientists are not really sure why we dream. Some scientists think dreams help build memories. Dreams also help us practice big feelings, so we understand them better when we feel them in real life.

Can you normally remember your dreams when you wake up?

Bad dreams are called nightmares. Nightmares can feel very scary. If you have a nightmare, talk to your trusted grown-up. Talking about things that make you scared or worried can help you feel better.

A HEALTHY LIFESTYLE

Your lifestyle is the way that you live your life. It is made up of all the things you do each day. Getting plenty of sleep is just one important part of a healthy lifestyle.

Drinking plenty of water, eating <u>nutritious</u> foods, keeping warm, and exercising are also important parts of a healthy lifestyle. Exercising during the day can help you feel tired enough to sleep well at night.

THANKING YOUR BODY

Your body is your home, and it will be for your whole life. Thanking your body means noticing everything your body does for you and thanking it for working so hard.

What will you thank your body for today?

Caring for your body is another way that you can thank it for everything is does. Taking care of your body will help to keep your body and mind healthy.

What will you do to care for your body today?

GLOSSARY

anxious a feeling of worry or nervousness

body clock something in the brain that controls when a person feels tired or hungry

cells tiny parts that make up all living things

energy the power that makes living things able to move and live

infections illnesses caused by dirt, germs, and bacteria getting into the body

nutritious contains lots of nutrients that people need to live, grow, and stay healthy

one-third one of three equal parts of one whole

recover to feel better after something challenging

supply a stored amount of something

trusted describing someone you can trust and feel safe with

INDEX